EMPOWERED

EMPOWERED

A Tale of Three Cities
Taking Charge of their Energy Future

By Bentham Paulos

Published by

MIDWEST ENERGY NEWS

with support from

ENERGY FOUNDATION
building a new energy future

Acknowledgements

For Jess, Jerome and Georgia, my team.

No book is written without help, especially this one.

Ken Paulman at *Midwest Energy News* was a judicious and thoughtful editor.

I give thanks to the activists and experts in Boulder, Minneapolis, and Wisconsin who generously explained the details of their work. Jonathan Koehn in Boulder, and John Farrell, Ken Bradley, and Mike Bull in Minneapolis were especially forthcoming. Special thanks are due to Chris Deisinger, Don Wichert, and Mitch Brey of RePower Madison, and Andy Olsen of the Environmental Law & Policy Center.

I would also like to thank the hard work of the many local journalists who are covering developments in energy. I relied heavily on coverage from the *Daily Camera* in Boulder, the Minneapolis *Star Tribune* and *MinnPost* in Minnesota, and the *Milwaukee Journal Sentinel*, the *Shepherd Express*, the *LaCrosse Tribune*, the *Capitol Times* and *The Isthmus* in Wisconsin. (And of course, *Midwest Energy News*, the premier energy news source for the region.) Erica Meltzer at the *Daily Camera* and Thomas Content at the *Journal Sentinel* were especially invaluable. I take all responsibility for errors of fact, interpretation, and omission.

With gratitude, *Midwest Energy News* thanks Sharon Grimes for her time and expertise in support of this project.

Cover photo © Emma Cassidy, Survival Media Agency

Midwest Energy News (www.midwestenergynews.com) is an online news service published by the RE-AMP network and Fresh Energy in St. Paul, Minnesota.

Bentham Paulos can be reached at PaulosAnalysis.com, and is on Twitter at @benpaulos.

Contents

Chapter 1:
The best of times,
the worst of times

In the world of clean energy, these are the best of times and these are the worst of times.

Renewable energy technologies, long the domain of off-the-grid cabins, early adopters, and tinkerers, have become cost-effective and potent, and their use is growing rapidly worldwide.

Energy demand is leveling off in the United States and Europe, as more efficient vehicles, appliances, and buildings allow for a high standard of living with less energy waste.

The computer revolution has brought us new energy technologies with embedded intelligence that can be controlled with software programs to respond to changing prices. Solid state electronics have made lighting wildly more efficient, long-lasting, and affordable.

These changes hold out the hope of real progress on global warming, the fundamental illness of our modern industrial civilization.

Yet these are also the worst of times.

As changes sweep through the energy sector, the incumbent energy industries, including some of the largest companies in the world, are pushing back. Pouring billions of dollars into campaign contributions, lobbying, propaganda, and litigation, they are seeking to prevent action on global warming, and to protect their profits.

Their efforts are bearing fruit, as partisan splits on energy and the environment become wider, bringing action in Congress to a halt and threatening progress in the states.

For citizens concerned about the fate of the planet, the options for effecting change through government action seem to be narrowing. If Congress is closed, and the states are too passive, what can be done?

In cities such as Boulder, Minneapolis, and Madison, a major part of the solution has been local action. While these cities – and many others – had established important-sounding sustainability goals, their ability to influence the energy use of their citizens was limited. State and federal governments are typically responsible for energy policy, not cities. And if you can't clean up your energy supply, it's far more difficult to address climate change.

But where there is a will, there is a way.

Inspired by the Kyoto Protocol, Boulder had committed to reduce carbon emissions, and was making good progress on parts of their sustainability plan.

But Jonathan Koehn, the city sustainability director, said that electricity, provided by coal-heavy Xcel Energy, was a major problem.

"We concluded that we had to clean up the power supply," he said. "Unfortunately, Xcel wasn't willing to go very far."

When negotiations with Xcel proved unfruitful, Boulder embarked on a "hostile takeover" of the power system, exercising their public authority to provide utility services. Years of litigation and wrangling have resulted, but they are making progress.

In Minneapolis, the goals are the same, but the dynamic has been different so far.

Xcel also serves the city of Minneapolis, where it has its headquarters. While Xcel's relations were better in Minneapolis than in Boulder, citizen activists were frustrated that the utility was doing little to help the city reach its climate goals. With Xcel's franchise agreement coming up for renewal, citizens launched a grassroots campaign to see whether the contract could be leveraged to reduce carbon emissions. Although full-on municipalization was considered, the campaign focused on a range of options to allow a more open-ended discussion.

Inspired no doubt by their contentious experience in Boulder, Xcel quickly reached an agreement with Minneapolis officials (and so did Centerpoint, the natural gas utility). The parties have launched a partnership to pursue local energy efficiency and renewable energy projects, bringing a cleaner environment and local jobs to the community.

The process has just started and it is too soon to say whether it will succeed. It could become a national model for how cities can work with utilities to address their electric and gas carbon emissions. Or it could be the first step in the long and frustrating path that Boulder has walked.

Perhaps the greatest frustration has been felt in Madison. A political revolution led by Governor Scott Walker is transforming what had been a traditionally moderate state into a bastion of conservatism and, many critics would argue, corporate influence. While fights with labor unions have attracted national press coverage, the agenda also includes energy.

Wisconsin has become a major battleground in a national push by utilities and their trade groups against broader adoption of efficiency and clean energy. As customers become more energy efficient and generate their own power with solar panels, electricity sales are stagnating, crimping the profits of power companies. Utilities are pushing regulators to let them change the way customers pay for service, increasing the fixed portion of their bills. This would guarantee that the money keeps flowing, even if less power is sold. It would also discourage customers from being more efficient or using solar power.

While regulators in most states have rejected such proposals as punitive, in Wisconsin they were welcomed, even encouraged. Madison Gas & Electric (MGE) proposed hiking charges from $10 to $69 a month, igniting a firestorm of protest. Milwaukee-based We Energies imposed new fees and penalties on customers with solar panels, taking away almost half the value of existing investments.

Political leaders were outspoken in their opposition.

MGE has "spent a lot of money on their image, as a 'leading green corporation'," said Madison city councilman David Ahrens. "The greenwash is endless. But MGE is not a green corporation."

Milwaukee leaders had a similar reaction. "Clearly we do not have a utility that is regulated in the public interest anymore," Alderman Robert Bauman said. "Something has to give in this relationship with the utility and the city of Milwaukee."

The experience of local leaders and citizen activists in Boulder and Minneapolis is providing inspiration and ideas for next steps in Wisconsin.

"That stuff in Minneapolis and Boulder is exciting," Ahrens said. "It's clear that the state won't help us. The only matter is to what degree they will cripple all efforts at the local level."

"Today in Wisconsin the responsibility for promoting clean energy has become the domain of cities," pointed out Madison Mayor Paul Soglin.

Chapter 2:
Corporate resistance
to climate action

T he frustration of citizens and local elected officials can be best understood against a backdrop of growing concern about the environmental impacts of energy production, most notably climate change, and nonstop lobbying against clean energy and climate policies by the most polluting industries and their front groups. This onslaught has nearly paralyzed government action.

Boulder, Minneapolis, and Madison are just a few of many cities and states that find their environmental goals to be out of step with the profit motives of the utilities that serve them.

Environmental impacts

The environmental impacts of energy are becoming more clear every day. The last five years have seen a steady stream of disasters and controversy, and increasingly clear science.

Coal may be the king of environmental impacts. Burning coal for electricity is the single largest source of carbon dioxide emissions, accounting for 77 percent of all power plant emissions and 20 percent of emissions from all sources. And despite advances in air pollution control technology, coal plants still emit pollutants such as nitrogen oxide, sulfur dioxide, mercury, and even small amounts of radiation.

Ironically, the air pollution controls are leading to other problems. To capture air pollution, coal power plants use giant filters to scrub out particulates, and gypsum to remove acid gases, both creating large quantities of toxic waste. This waste has typically been stored in large containment ponds, with earthen sides, unlined on the bottom and open to the rain on top. Thanks to heavy rains, the sides of the ponds have failed, dumping massive amounts of toxic sludge into rivers. There are over 1,000 of these earthen ponds in the United States, holding billions of tons of waste accumulated over the decades. Although the biggest spills have been in North Carolina and Tennessee, numerous incidents have occurred, including a bluff collapse at a We Energies coal power plant in 2011 that spilled 2,500 cubic yards of coal ash into Lake Michigan.[1]

Although the grid is getting cleaner, utilities in Wisconsin, Minnesota, and Colorado, as in most states, are still heavily dependent on coal, as will be outlined in later chapters.

The oil industry has a comparable reputation when it comes to the environment. Oil accounts for the bulk of carbon emissions and is the primary contributor to smog in many cities around the world. In addition to these chronic problems, it creates regular headlines when it is spilled – a particular concern in Colorado, which remains one of the top oil-producing states in the United States; and Minnesota and Wisconsin, which are criss-crossed by pipelines and rail lines carrying crude from North Dakota and Alberta to Midwest refineries. In recent years there have been over 100 oil train accidents per year, including a fiery 21-car derailment near scenic Galena, Illinois, that dumped oil into the Mississippi River.[2]

As conventional oil and gas supplies run out, companies are turning to hydraulic fracturing, known as fracking. In fracking, oil and gas companies drill down into "tight oil" formations, then hammer a cocktail of water, sand, and chemicals down the hole under great pressure, forcing cracks in the shale to release oil and gas.

Fracking has led to a host of environmental concerns. Drinking and irrigation water has been contaminated by poorly sealed drill holes. Rivers and streams have been polluted as companies improperly dispose of contaminated wastewater. Wastewater injected underground has caused earthquakes – notably in places like Oklahoma that rarely see earthquakes, but also in Colorado, where state regulators have shut down injection wells because of increased seismic activity. According to the U.S. Geological Survey, there were typically about 21 earthquakes per year in the central United States. With the advent of fracking, the number skyrocketed to 659 in 2014.[3]

Special sand used in fracking operations is heavily mined in Wisconsin, and to a lesser extent in Minnesota. Wisconsin produces half the nation's frac sand, with at least 63 active sand mines, 45 processing facilities, and 27 railroad loading facilities. Five years ago, there were just five mines and five processing plants.[4]

Other recent concerns are Canadian tar sands and the Keystone XL and other pipelines proposed to link them to U.S. refineries and ports. Tar sands are like naturally occurring asphalt, where thick crude oil is mixed with sand. Extracting them means scraping the surface of all plant life, loading the mix into trucks, then heating it to liquefy and drain out the oil. The process is highly energy intensive and polluting, and destroys the landscape. Koch Industries is heavily invested in tar sands, with over 1 million acres of land under contract.[5]

The resulting high-sulfur crude is sent to refineries in Alberta and the United States via long distance pipelines, including the Flint Hills refinery south of Minneapolis, owned by Koch Industries. That refinery produces 30 to 40 percent of Wisconsin's gasoline, much sold through Kwik Trip stores, as well as jet fuel sold to the Minneapolis-St. Paul Airport.[6]

But the biggest environmental concern by far is global warming.

Scientists have known about the greenhouse effect since the 1800s, recognizing that carbon dioxide plays a critical role in retaining heat in the earth's atmosphere. In 1896, Swedish scientist Svante Arrhenius calculated that a "doubling of the percentage of carbon dioxide in the air would raise the temperature of the earth's surface by 4° C."[7]

In more recent decades, increasingly sophisticated science has brought into sharper resolution the impact that man's dependence on fossil fuels is having on the climate – a fact that even major oil companies like Shell and ExxonMobil openly acknowledge.

Yet the fossil fuel industries – coal, oil, and gas producers, electric utilities, and car makers – have also for years denied and obfuscated the science of climate change. Science historian Naomi Oreskes, in her book Merchants of Doubt, documented a band of activists who were paid to cast doubt on issues that would affect their corporate benefactors. For four decades they claimed that the science of global warming was "not settled," and denied the findings of studies linking smoking to lung cancer, coal emissions to acid rain, and chlorofluorocarbons (CFCs) to the ozone hole.

"Doubt is our product," wrote one tobacco executive quoted in the book.

Political fights

Despite this growing concern about the impacts of energy, there is little consensus among policymakers about what action to take, thanks to the massive political influence and funding of the polluting industries and their front groups. Numerous battles have been fought, and are ongoing, at the state and federal level.

The most notable battle was around national climate legislation proposed by Reps. Henry Waxman and Ed Markey in 2009. The bill would have placed a cap on carbon emissions, with polluters allowed to trade emission allowances to find the most cost-effective reductions. While it passed the House, it was never brought for a vote in the Senate, thanks to a filibuster.

The bill inspired opponents of climate action to spend an estimated $500 million on lobbying, advertising, and campaign contributions. Oil and gas companies accounted for six of the top seven spenders on lobbying and campaign contributions during this period, with ExxonMobil number one.[8]

But the battle over the Markey-Waxman bill was not the end of the war. The U.S. Supreme Court has ruled that the Environmental Protection Agency (EPA), under the authority of the Clean Air Act, can regulate carbon emissions. The EPA's Clean Power Plan seeks to cut global warming pollution from existing power plants about 30 percent below 2005 levels by 2030. The plan would give states the flexibility to implement a wide variety of policies, including energy efficiency, fuel switching, and renewable energy, building on existing policies and trends. The EPA expects the rule would deliver public health and climate benefits worth an estimated $34 billion to $54 billion per year in 2030, far outweighing the costs of $8.4 billion.[9]

But the plan has met staunch opposition from congressional Republicans, industry, and a number of states led by Republican governors – including Scott Walker of Wisconsin. Senate Majority Leader Mitch McConnell has gone so far as to urge states not to comply with the plan.

"Don't be complicit in the administration's attack on the middle class," he said in an op-ed in the *Lexington Herald-Leader*.[10]

The polluting industries and their allies in government are planning a full-on legal assault as well.[11] At least 15 predominantly Republican-led states will challenge the regulations, and hundreds of trade groups, utilities, and coal and power companies are expected to join their effort, making it one of the most heavily litigated environmental regulations ever.

So far only 11 states have regulated carbon pollution, including California and a cluster in the Northeast known as the Regional Greenhouse Gas Initiative (RGGI). But many more states have adopted carbon-reducing policies, especially in the electricity sector.

More than 30 states have adopted renewable energy mandates – including Minnesota, Wisconsin, and Colorado – while 24 have set energy efficiency standards requiring utilities to hit energy saving goals. Practically all states offer tax incentives or other favorable policies, to varying degrees.

Polluting industries and their allies have begun to attack state policies as well. In a coordinated action, the American Legislative Exchange Council (ALEC), Americans for Prosperity (AFP), the Heartland Institute, and local members of the State Policy Network have sought to undermine renewable energy and energy efficiency laws in numerous states.

So far, they have failed to repeal many of their targeted policies, but they have succeeded in making clean energy a highly partisan issue.

This is now being reinforced by the Koch brothers, Charles and David, the American industrialists who are among the richest men in the world with a combined worth of almost $100 billion. The Kochs have announced that their political network will be spending $889 million in the 2016 presidential campaign, an amount equal to the Republican and Democratic parties.[12]

This has had a powerful effect on the race already. All of the current or expected Republican candidates either deny the science behind climate change, reject any action to reduce carbon emissions, or both.[13]

The Kochs' presidential pledge comes on top of the large and unknown amounts they spend influencing races for Congress and at the state and local level. Since much of their giving is suspected to go through secretive "dark money " funds like Donor's Trust, the full extent of their influence is not known.[14]

The Kochs are major funders of various political activist groups as well, like ALEC, Americans for Prosperity (AFP), and the Heartland Institute, both directly and through intermediate groups. David Koch is on the board of AFP, for example, and they are the largest recipient of funds from Donor's Trust.

But the Kochs are not the only source of opposition to climate action. ExxonMobil, the world's largest oil and gas company, has long funded anti-science climate activists such as the Heartland Institute and the Institute for Energy Research.

The National Association of Manufacturers (NAM), the U.S. Chamber of Commerce, and Edison Electric Institute (EEI) are additional pillars of opposition.

Power sector fights

EEI has become especially active fighting state clean energy policies. The trade association of investor-owned utilities, EEI has organized and supported member utilities to undermine state laws encouraging customers to produce their own solar and wind energy. Over 40 states allow customers to roll their meter backward when their energy system produces more than they need, then buy power from the utility when it produces less, a practice known as net metering.

EEI is concerned that as solar power becomes more affordable, more customers will find it cost effective to produce their own power. This will cut into their revenues and create a new and unwelcome form of competition. And because the utility still has fixed investments like power plants, wires, and meters to pay for, they argue that those fixed costs will have to be paid by an ever-shrinking base of customers.

At the same time, electricity demand seems to have plateaued, with essentially no growth since 2007. Although the Great Recession in 2008 likely contributed, demand has not come back as the economy revived, because consumers are becoming more energy efficient. New technologies, new government standards, utility efficiency programs and incentives, and new industrial processes are all contributing to a growth rate expected to remain well below one percent per year for the next 25 years.[15]

A third factor is that information technologies have enabled consumers to become active participants in grid operations. Internet and wireless communications, smart controls, and data analysis have made it possible for utilities and other companies to track and control demand at an unprecedented level. Customers are now able to modify their usage, often using automatic controls such as internet-enabled thermostats, to respond to price signals and provide valuable services to grid operators, ramping up and down in the same way power plants can.

All of these are contributing to a disruptive challenge to the traditional utility business model. In the old way of doing business, utilities generated power and sold it to captive customers, with demand – and profits – ever-increasing. Now, it is increasingly a two-way street, with customers and their software-controlled systems actively participating and even competing with utilities to provide grid services.

For this reason, leading states have begun to change the rules to transform utilities into neutral platforms for innovation, letting customers and entrepreneurs try new approaches while the utility acts as the grid manager. Proceedings in New York, California, Minnesota, and elsewhere promise to create an entirely new business model for the 21st century.

But many utilities are not eager to innovate. In a January 2013 report for EEI called *Disruptive Challenges*, consultant Peter Kind laid out a dire scenario of distributed solar leading to a financial "death spiral" for utilities.[16] While the report became famous as a validation of new technologies and led to an active discussion about utility business models, it also gave advice on how utilities could stop new technologies from disrupting their business models.

Kind cautioned EEI that solar "is not the only disruptive risk the industry faces. Energy efficiency and DSM (demand-side management) programs that promote lower electricity sales pressure earnings required to support capital investment."

"Investors have no desire to sit by and watch as disruptive forces slice away at the value and financial prospects of their investment," the paper noted.

"When utility investors become focused on these new risks and start to witness significant customer and earnings erosion trends, they will respond to these challenges. But, by then, it may be too late to repair the utility business model."

Instead, utilities must "address these challenges early on so that uneconomic disruption does not proceed further."

At the top of the list for recommended action is "Institute a monthly customer service charge to all tariffs in all states."

Utilities, with the help of EEI, are now following this playbook. They are seeking changes in rate design that will accomplish two goals: first, to insulate themselves from lost sales and revenues by guaranteeing their profits regardless of volume, and second, to slow down revenue losses by making it less attractive for customers to reduce demand.

Utilities have proposed these changes in over a dozen states so far. Arizona's largest utility, Arizona Public Service, spent $9 million – more than was spent by every 2010 gubernatorial candidate combined – opposing incentives for solar power.[17] This included $3.7 million in campaign-style television advertising in only three months. APS was seeking to impose a $50 per month penalty on any customer with a solar panel. The effort even involved funding front groups like the 60 Plus Association, a conservative alternative to the AARP, funded almost entirely by the Koch-backed political funds Freedom Partners and American Encore.

Although most state regulators have rejected these proposals, a few have been approved. One of the most drastic, as described later, was in Wisconsin, where regulators urged utilities to ask for massive increases in fixed charges and new taxes on solar customers. Some self-regulating utilities, like the Salt River Project in Arizona, have also adopted new fees, over the objections of their customer-owners.

Given the level of influence that corporate polluters have on political parties and Congress, and the attacks on state policy, concerned citizens are increasingly asking what can be done in their local communities.

To Ken Bradley, an environmental activist in Minneapolis, the path was clear.

"To really solve climate you really have to solve it at the local and state level," he says. "We have such an inept Congress."

Chapter 3:
The tale of Boulder

Nestled against the front range of the Rocky Mountains, Boulder, Colorado, a city of 111,000 residents, is an ideal place for local action. The local culture is permeated with a love of nature, fostered by outdoor activities like skiing and cycling. It was rated the #1 Sports Town in America by Outside Magazine, and is a training spot for many top professional athletes.

The Boulder area is also crawling with energy and climate experts, working at the National Renewable Energy Laboratory, the National Wind Technology Center, the National Oceanic and Atmospheric Administration (NOAA), and the National Center for Atmospheric Research, a leading climate research lab.

So if any community is going to demand a cleaner energy supply, it would be here. Boulder activists and local officials have been talking about and studying options to be cleaner for decades, according to city sustainability coordinator Jonathan Koehn.

"The concept has come up with every franchise renewal, every 20 years," he said. "It's the one chance a community has to negotiate."

A franchise agreement is the permission that a city grants to a utility to use city property, like streets and sidewalks, to site power poles and other equipment. Cities usually receive a small payment from the utility, funded by utility customers. They are regulated by state laws and vary from state to state. The agreements typically last for many years and are renewed with little fanfare.

But negotiations this time around came to an impasse, and Boulder is now attempting to start a municipal utility to supply electricity to the homes and businesses of the city.

"The key driver behind this initiative is to reduce greenhouse gas emissions," said Heather Bailey, speaking to the Santa Cruz Chamber of Commerce in 2013.[18] Bailey is the executive director of Boulder Energy Future, the city effort to launch the utility.

"The current portfolio is 60 percent coal, and that is not acceptable," she said. "Boulder has a very aggressive climate action program, doing a lot of things with energy efficiency, demand side management, transportation. But at the end of the day, until you change where your power comes from, you can't make the kind of impact you need to make."

Boulder's power supply is delivered by Xcel Energy, a conglomerate serving customers in eight states. Xcel serves 60 percent of Colorado electricity demand, primarily from customers in the Denver area, through its Public Service of Colorado subsidiary (PSCO).

The state has already established some of the more aggressive energy efficiency and renewable energy policies in the country. According to the Southwest Energy Efficiency Partnership (SWEEP), Xcel spent $75 million on energy efficiency programs in 2013, which are expected to yield $160 million in net benefits.[19] Overall, the state was ranked 13th in the nation by the American Council for an Energy Efficient Economy (ACEEE) in 2014.[20]

The state also has a substantial renewable electricity standard, requiring investor-owned utilities like Xcel to get 30 percent of their power from renewables by 2020. Originally approved by a statewide ballot initiative in 2004, it was later expanded and extended by the legislature.

As a result, Xcel got 19 percent of its electricity from wind power in 2014, with an additional 3 percent from solar and hydroelectric power.[21] Xcel has been the nation's top utility wind power provider for 11 years running, according to the American Wind Energy Association (AWEA). The company also had about 320 megawatts of solar power on their system as of June 2014, primarily in Colorado.

But Xcel still gets the majority of its power from fossil fuel plants, including 13 plants throughout its territory running on coal and 27 running on natural gas. In 2014, Xcel's resource mix was 53 percent coal, and 25 percent natural gas. That is improving, but slowly, as the company still anticipates getting 71 percent from fossil fuels by 2020.

Overall, Colorado has the 10th highest emissions rate for CO2, at 1,647 pounds per megawatt-hour (MWh).[22] Xcel's Colorado subsidiary is slightly cleaner at 1,516 pounds per MWh.[23]

Xcel has also been less than enthusiastic about the growth of customer-owned solar, according to Vote Solar, a solar advocacy organization. In 2013, Xcel proposed a drastic revision of net metering policies that allow businesses and homeowners to be reimbursed for excess energy they send back to the grid.

"Instead of engaging in a thoughtful conversation about how the solar industry and Xcel can work together to make rooftop solar an important and a more valuable part of their power supply mix, Xcel is simply trying to get rid of what they see as competition – customer generated solar power," they wrote.[24]

There are over 19,000 customers with solar in Colorado, and more than 387 solar companies at work throughout the value chain in Colorado, employing 4,200 people, according to the Solar Energy Industries Association.

Still, Xcel is far from the worst utility in the country. "It's not like we've got a 100-percent coal mix. We're a very progressive, environmental-leaning utility," Xcel regional vice president Jerome Davis told GovExec State & Local.[25] "Boulder's been the first city that's entered into this under a different sort of a theme − a theme of renewables or carbon reduction. That's what's so odd about this."

"Xcel is not a terrible company, and we've never said they were," said Jonathan Koehn, Boulder's sustainability director. "It's their business model that is the problem." As long as the utility industry profits from selling more electricity and building more power plants and infrastructure, he thinks they will be opposed to helping customers reduce demand and generate their own power.

The bottom line, according to Boulder city officials and activists, is that Xcel is simply not doing enough. Inspired by the 1992 Kyoto Treaty, the City of Boulder in 2002 adopted a goal of reducing carbon emissions 7 percent below 1990 levels by 2012.

"Our community supports the creation of a local electric utility because of its commitment to moving to a cleaner energy supply, and a city-owned utility would make that transition a core value and priority," said Heather Bailey.

"The carbon-intensity of the power supply, that's what gets the young people out to vote, and they are a very strong voting bloc," Bailey told GovExec. "The whole issue of emissions, of climate change in their future, they take that very seriously."

Boulder has strong efficiency and transportation programs, and even has a carbon tax, approved by voters in 2006. But Koehn said their climate action plan was only taking them so far without addressing the source of electricity.

As noted in a report on their Climate Action Plan, "Boulder has made progress in slowing the growth of greenhouse gas emissions, but we will not meet our Kyoto Protocol goal by 2012 as originally hoped. This is largely because Colorado has one of the most carbon-intensive sources of electricity in the country."[26]

"We are aggressive on the demand side but can't do anything on the supply side," Koehn said. "We wanted to set carbon reduction goals post-2012, but we were fighting against the current of Xcel bringing new fossil units online, making carbon intensity go up. That meant we had to go back to residents to say they have to conserve more because Xcel's carbon intensity is going up. That was a hard message to deliver, especially to businesses who want to grow."

"We concluded that we had to clean up the power supply," added Koehn. "Unfortunately, Xcel wasn't willing to go very far."

> **Boulder is working to "Democratize, Decentralize, and Decarbonize" their power supply.**
>
> This means, according to the City:
>
> • **Democratize Energy Decision Making**: Boulder customers should have more direct control and involvement in decisions about their energy, including opportunities to invest in their long-term energy needs and to have a say in energy investments made on their behalf.
> • **Decentralize Energy Generation and Management**: Energy should be generated locally or within the region to the maximum extent feasible, reducing reliance on external fuel sources; customers should be able to manage and reduce their energy use as directly and effectively as possible; and energy service companies should be empowered to compete and innovate within a diverse and robust local energy economy.
> • **Decarbonize the Energy Supply**: Renewable and clean fuel sources should be maximized as much as possible, as quickly as possible, minimizing both short- and long-term environmental impacts and maximizing energy independence over time.

The municipalization effort actually began as early as 2002, when Boulder kicked off a climate action campaign. By 2005, the city commissioned a "preliminary municipalization" study from engineering firm RW Beck, in anticipation of renewing their franchise agreement in 2010. The study estimated the cost of Boulder acquiring Xcel's distribution system in the city at between $93 million and $123 million, and that there were no significant barriers.

In 2006, voters approved the city's climate action plan and a carbon tax to fund it. Susan Osborne was a city councilor and mayor of Boulder starting in 2007.

"When I came on the city council, I had no interest in municipalizing even though it was a nascent issue when I was elected," she said at an event in Minneapolis in 2012. "It took quite a while for me to get to the point where municipalization was a real option and something we should explore."

She pointed to a number of half-hearted efforts Xcel made to address the city's desires. In 2008, they launched a pilot program called Smart Grid City that would make Boulder a showcase for new smart grid technologies.

"We thought it was an excellent opportunity to work with Xcel on something that would revolutionize how we consume energy," said Shaun McGrath, Boulder's mayor at the time. The city council agreed to put aside consideration of municipalization, since Xcel was concerned about investing in a city that might leave their system.

Xcel's plan for Smart Grid City was to deploy thousands of sensors and smart meters that would enable tens of thousands of homes to communicate with the utility, right down to thermostats and appliances, according to the *Denver Post*.[28] The total project would cost $100 million, with a variety of corporate partners picking up the bulk of the cost.

But Xcel made poor choices in technology, funding partners withdrew, and the project ran into huge cost overruns. In 2013, the utility commission refused to let Xcel recover $16.6 million of expenses from customers, citing the lack of customer benefits and the inability to justify expenditures.

By 2010, the franchise agreement expired with no agreement between the City and Xcel. The City adopted a local occupation tax on Xcel to replace the $3.5 million per year they had been receiving through the franchise agreement.

According to Mayor Osborne, Xcel also offered to develop a wind farm just for Boulder if the city would put a plain extension of the franchise agreement on the ballot, with no conditions. "Xcel changed their mind, I guess," she told a crowd in Minneapolis. "We never really understood what happened."

The council unanimously rejected the idea of a no-condition extension.

Instead the city council put two items on the November 2011 ballot giving the city the right to municipalize, with bonding power up to a certain amount, and set standards that would have to be met before municipalizing. One condition was that rates for the municipal system would have to be at or below Xcel rates.

"It was a horrendously hard-fought election," Osborne recalled. "Xcel spent a lot of money trying to defeat municipalization in Boulder. Our citizen group had to raise money and conduct their own campaign. It was really a cliff hanger. In the end voters approved both ballot measures by just a hair."

Xcel retaliated in 2013, funding a citizen initiative to add a kill pill to the municipalization plan by putting impossibly strong limitations on it. The city council responded by proposing a cost cap for acquiring Xcel's local system. The city council measure passed, while Xcel's measure failed – by a much wider margin than the 2011 vote.

Now the city had to prove it could provide power at the same rate and same reliability, but with more renewables and fewer emissions. The overall budget cap was set at $214 million.

This kicked off another round of analysis to see if charter requirements could be met. Working groups involved over 100 people, including local experts on energy and climate change. The analysis concluded the city could meet the conditions, with 50 percent renewable energy at same price and reliability.

With the analysis in hand, the city council adopted an ordinance in May 2014 formally announcing the creation of a municipal electric utility and filed a petition in court seeking to acquire Xcel's local distribution system. "This action starts the countdown to startup of a city-owned electric utility," they noted at the time.

The process will have two landmarks. "Day 1" will be the date the city takes ownership of the electric system and begins customer billing, sometime in 2017. "Day 2" will be when a new interconnection with the rest of the grid is finished, late in 2018. The City may collaborate with Xcel during the transition.

But first, the City and Xcel need to settle on a price to be paid for the utility's assets. The state utility commission will judge the value of assets, which Koehn estimates at between $120 million and

$150 million. The Federal Energy Regulatory Commission will decide the value of any stranded costs – investments made by Xcel that are lost in the process of municipalization. Boulder would have to pay for those as well.

In ads run in opposition to the 2011 referendum, Xcel dismissed Boulder's cost estimate for the transition, citing over a billion dollars that they would be owed, including such extras as "Going Concern."[29]

"Going Concern is the amount the city would owe the company for replacing future lost revenue," the ad explained. "Stranded Cost is the amount Boulder would owe Xcel Energy for economic damages associated with having acquired electric generation to serve Boulder. And Program Investments is what the city would owe Xcel Energy and other customers who have funded programs in which Boulder customers participate."

Koehn dismisses this as a tactic to scare voters around the 2011 ballot measure. Negotiations since then have narrowed the gap, as has depreciation.

The city also budgeted $2.3 million per year for the municipalization effort in 2014, though legal challenges from Xcel may push the cost higher. And the legal wrangling shows no sign of stopping. Because some of the distribution equipment serving Boulder is outside city limits, Xcel sued to stop the process. A court ruling in February temporarily halted the condemnation proceedings until the state PUC has had a chance to act.

Still, there are signs that a future relationship is emerging. Boulder released a request for proposals to sell power to the new city power system. Xcel responded favorably.[30]

"Tapping Xcel for wholesale power at the outset, and then diminishing our purchase over time, is an option that ensures a smooth transition between the utilities, minimizes potential disruptions in service, and supports the immediate needs of our customers," according to Heather Bailey.

"We see this as a win-win," Koehn told Fierce Energy.[31]

"Out of the gate, a local electric utility could continue to buy power from Xcel, which would be reassuring to customers and the Public Utilities Commission for those early days during the transition," he said. "Then the city could gradually depart the system as we transform to the modern fossil-fuel-free utility our community wants. This has the added benefit of

Here's a summary of the range of utility start-up costs as estimated by the city and by UtiliPoint.**		
(costs in millions of dollars)	Boulder	Possible
Assets	$121	$150
Separation Cost	$15	$100+
Start-up	$45	$45
Going Concern	$0	$350
Stranded Cost	$0	$335
Program Investments (SmartGridCity®/Energy Efficiency/Solar*Rewards®)	$0	$100
Financing Costs (cash reserves, interest, debt service, underwriting)	$105	$106
TOTAL	$286 million	?

Figure 1: Xcel estimate of utility startup costs, an ad from the 2011 ballot campaign

protecting other Xcel customers as our departure could coincide with Xcel's need for additional power in the future."

While Xcel is eager to sell power to the new utility, they would prefer to remain the city's utility.

"We remain steadfast in our goals of carbon reduction and the use of renewable energy, which aligns with Boulder's stated environmental goals," the utility said in a recent statement.[32]

"By working together, we can provide customers with options that take advantage of our mutual strengths. We continue to believe that this is the optimal path for success," the utility said.

Lessons learned

Koehn cited a number of lessons from Boulder's experience so far.

"We thought talking and voting on municipalization would bring utilities to the table in a meaningful way. We thought they would say fine, we realize you are serious."

But the current utility business model doesn't reward utilities for being responsive to consumers who want to save energy or produce their own, he said. The result has been a years-long fight.

Still, he advised perseverance. "Don't underestimate the power citizens have in changing the business model," he said. "Be forthcoming about your goals, have a clear focus on them. Don't roll over at the first opposition. Make the utility work to prove they should continue to provide the service. Be open to options that achieve the goals."

"The more communities that are vocal about the needs and wants of their customers, the quicker we get to the point where utilities will transform," he said. "Evolve or die."

Chapter 4:
The tale of Minneapolis

The movement toward local control in Boulder did not go unnoticed in Minneapolis, partly because the same utility serves both cities. While Xcel Energy serves customers in Colorado and other states, it is headquartered in downtown Minneapolis. The company serves customers in Minnesota, North Dakota, and Wisconsin through its Northern States Power subsidiary.

As in Boulder, Minneapolis officials and many citizens have long wanted to do more to reduce carbon pollution. R.T. Rybak, the mayor of Minneapolis from 2001 to 2012, was a leader in creating the Mayor's Climate Protection Agreement in 2005.[33] Ultimately 1,060 mayors from all 50 states, representing over 88 million citizens, signed the pledge.

"I felt I had a real mandate from the residents of my city, and we needed to send a message – especially since our country didn't sign the Kyoto Accord," he told the U.S. Conference of Mayors in 2009.

"The fact that more than 1,000 mayors signed the agreement was much more than I hoped for. Now, I think we need to go even further and demand more and greater action."

Still, Rybak and other civic leaders were frustrated that some of the most important sources of carbon pollution were beyond their ability to influence. Although the city developed policies and programs to encourage better urban planning, transit and bicycle use, community gardens, and many other activities, there was little they could do to reduce carbon emissions from electricity and natural gas production, which account for two-thirds of the total. State and federal governments have jurisdiction over these utilities.

Like Colorado, Minnesota has some substantial state policies to encourage clean energy. Minnesota was the first state outside of California to see significant wind power development, thanks to a 1994 settlement about storage of radioactive waste from Xcel's Prairie Island nuclear power plant. The deal required 825 MW of wind and 125 MW of biomass to be developed by the end of 2002, in exchange for allowing 17 casks of radioactive waste to be stored at the plant.

The success of the first wind farms, plus growing concern about climate change, led to major legislation in 2007. The Next Generation Energy Act, signed by Republican governor Tim Pawlenty, set goals for cutting the state's greenhouse gas emissions to 15 percent below 2005 levels by 2015, 30 percent by 2025 and 80 percent by 2050. It also created a 25 percent renewable power standard in 2007. Xcel is subject to a higher standard of 31.5 percent by 2020 to account for the Prairie Island deal.

The law also set an energy efficiency target of saving 1.5 percent of demand each year. Minnesota has been a leading Midwestern state for energy efficiency for many years, ranking 10th nationally in ACEEE's 2014 rating.

While much was happening at the state level, progress in Minneapolis was slower than city officials and climate action advocates wanted. John Farrell and Ken Bradley were two, working with the Institute for Local Self Reliance and Environment Minnesota, respectively. They and others started meeting in 2012.

"For me, the motivation was to solve the climate issue and get solar and local energy to occur," said Bradley. "Then I read about what was going on in Boulder."

"Both cities were in similar situations in that they've established these (climate) goals, and they have agreements with utilities that may not share those goals," he said.[34]

As in Boulder, Xcel's franchise agreement with Minneapolis was coming up for renewal. As part of their franchise agreements, Xcel and the gas utility CenterPoint Energy were paying $23 million into the city's general fund.

But the bulk of the money citizens spend on electricity and gas, about $450 million a year, leaves the local economy to pay for fuel, equipment, and services. "A lot of our energy decisions and our energy money are leaving our community," said Farrell, speaking at a meeting in October 2012.

"Lesson number one from Boulder is that these franchise agreement renewals are pretty critical moments," Bradley said. The advocates focused on the franchise agreement as an opportunity to get more attention on clean energy and carbon reductions from Xcel. They launched a campaign to explore what the options might be, called Minneapolis Energy Options (MEO).

Advocates figured the City had three strategic choices. They could renew the franchise agreement without any changes, accepting the status quo. Or they could use the franchise agreement to negotiate for more energy efficiency and clean energy. Or they could look at municipalization to gain more control, as Boulder did.

Although the votes in Boulder became a public referendum on Xcel's reputation and popularity, the situation in Minneapolis wasn't there yet.

"Boulder had a history of trying to work with the utility and getting screwed," said Farrell. "If you've been screwed enough you'll be able to get the votes and be willing to pay more to make it happen."

"Xcel is viewed pretty well in Minnesota, so we were cautious about how we did messaging," said Bradley. Their tactics were different as a result. "We made the central focus climate change. Xcel was less important."

Compared to Boulder, they downplayed municipalization as a goal. "We made municipalization the backdrop," said Bradley. "Instead of business as usual, we said let's look at all the options. The name 'Minneapolis Energy Options' underlined that it was all about options, not about attacking Xcel."

The options included working with the utilities.

"We didn't want to portray Xcel as the bad guy if they were willing to help us," Bradley said. "Our campaign goals look an awful lot like Boulder's," said Farrell in 2012. "We want clean, reliable, affordable, and local energy. We think all of them are equally important components. We are not 100 percent about driving toward municipalization, but we want a menu of options as we pursue our clean energy goals."

The campaign started in 2012 with the formation of a coalition of neighborhood groups, local business associations, environmental justice and youth organizations, labor, and economic justice advocates.

The grassroots campaign began in 2013 to push the city government to put an initiative on the ballot that would authorize (but not require) the formation of a city-owned utility. Through over 40 events, direct mail, and door-knocking, the campaign reached 65,000 Minneapolitans (out of 400,000 residents), became a central issue in the city council and mayoral elections, and garnered extensive media in the Twin Cities.

Environment Minnesota's sister organization, the Minnesota Public Interest Research Group (MPIRG), included the issue in their local door-knocking. "Anything to do with clean energy, people like it," Bradley recalled.

Although there was strong support on the city council in reducing carbon emissions, they were not ready to put the measure to authorize municipalization on the ballot. Instead, they developed an Energy Vision statement and commissioned an analysis of options.

"Some council members weren't convinced about winning a municipalization campaign but did want to know the options," Farrell said. "In some ways it was the first victory of the campaign, to get the city to put down their own money for a study."

The Energy Vision was a statement that "identifies the desired state of the Minneapolis energy system, where the goals of the city and its energy providers are aligned."[35]

"In 2040, Minneapolis's energy system will provide reliable, affordable, local, and clean energy services for Minneapolis homes, businesses, and institutions: sustaining the city's economy and environment and contributing to a more socially just community."

For the study of options, the City hired the Center for Energy and Environment (CEE), a Twin Cities energy think tank. Mike Bull, who had worked at Xcel during some of the Boulder fight, as well as with Gov. Pawlenty, led the study.

"The city was doing their climate action planning process, bringing all parties together, doing in-the-weeds analysis," he recalled. "At the same time, the franchise agreements were expiring in 18 months."

Bull credits Minneapolis Energy Options for putting the two together.

"They took the franchise seriously and worked on local officials to look at all the options for reducing carbon," he said. "Their public advocacy provided the want-to for whatever was going to get done. And their focus on options captured the attention of city officials and the public."

CEE came up with five pathways for the city, as shown in the box.[36]

The main innovation was a Clean Energy Partnership between the city and the utilities, where they would jointly set goals and oversee program implementation. Because state laws limit what can go in a franchise agreement, the agreement itself would be straightforward, but with shorter terms, and contingent on progress in other areas.

Other recommendations centered around influencing and leveraging state energy policies. For example, Minnesota law does not permit Community Choice Aggregation (CCA), which some call "muni-lite." Under CCA laws in six states, local governments can choose an electricity supplier for the whole community, without taking over the local grid or power plants. Over 650 cities and counties in Illinois, representing 80 percent of the residential power market, have chosen alternative suppliers under their CCA law.[37]

Cincinnati, for example, has chosen a 100 percent renewable mix, to be supplied by First Energy Solutions.

If Minnesota had CCA, Minneapolis could more easily green up their power supply, without going through the process of municipalization. CEE described municipalization as "the pathway that provides the city the greatest control over local energy services, as well as the greatest cost and risk."

"From the very beginning of 'public power,' the primary motivation was local control – local control over rates and services, and today, local control over the energy supply mix," the report says.

Center for Energy Efficiency
Clean Energy Pathways study for the City of Minneapolis

The study made five key recommendations:

1. Renew the City's utility franchise agreements with targeted enhancements, and for shorter terms. Traditionally and by law, franchise agreements have been limited to the subject of payment by utilities for the use of City rights-of-way for utility infrastructure. Because of statutory limitations in the use of franchise agreements, the study recommends that the scope of existing agreements be extended to cover some reporting, reliability, and right-of-way goals. However, these agreements should be of a shorter term, and renewal should be made contingent on satisfactory progress being made through additional agreements with the utilities.

2. Pursue additional, broader "Clean Energy Agreements" with utilities in which the City suspends its right to municipalize in exchange for utility commitment to meet the City's clean energy goals. These agreements would include the formation of a Clean Energy Coordinating Partnership, made up of City and utility leadership. This partnership would set program and policy goals, and help provide planning, leadership, coordination, promotion, and accountability for meeting these goals.

3. Use this Clean Energy Coordinating Partnership to leverage statewide policies, City municipal regulatory authority and community relationships, and utility expertise and funding to increase the penetration rate of efficiency and renewable energy, reliability, and equity of energy services in Minneapolis. Significant progress can be made on specific programs and policies to advance energy efficiency and renewable energy were the City to take full advantage of existing and enhanced utility programs in concert with specific City regulatory functions.

4. Continue to engage in state energy policy decisions that can improve the City's ability to meet its goals. Policy decisions made at the Public Utilities Commission, the Minnesota Department of Commerce, and Minnesota Legislature have a direct impact on energy outcomes. The City should continue to dedicate attention and resources to legislative issues, and participate in regulatory proceedings. Examples include legislation that clarifies the purpose and role of City-utility energy partner- ships, solar rate reform, utility resource planning, and data privacy and access.

5. Continue to pursue mid- and long-term options for increasing the City's control over its energy future. Pathways like Community Choice Aggregation (CCA) and municipalization offer the City the most control over its energy supply, albeit with greater risk, higher cost, and a longer timeframe. Should sufficient interest exist, the City should advocate for a detailed study of how CCA could operate in Minnesota and for changes to state law that would remove barriers to municipalization.

But Mike Bull thought the amount of effort involved in changing state law would be an impediment.

"The first two options required law changes and significant consternation and conflict at the Capitol," he said. "You weren't going to get progress soon, and you'd have to spend a lot of time fighting instead of meeting climate goals."

In the end, the report recommended a Clean Energy Partnership that would set clean energy goals and implement programs to achieve them. The franchise agreement would be extended for only five years, with an opportunity to renew for another five years, depending on progress.

"We thought we should try the partnership idea first," Bull said. "The city council absorbed the recommendation because it had the promise of making more progress more quickly, while holding out the option for other things.

"If this doesn't work, the other options are still on the table."

The deal was sealed in October 2014, when the city signed new franchise agreements with the utilities, accompanied by agreements that established the Clean Energy Partnership.[38]

"While each of the partners has achieved significant results independently, all three believe that greater results can be realized by thoughtfully combining their efforts," they said in announcing the agreement.

"This agreement signifies a new stage in our relationship with the utilities, marking our shared commitment to move toward clean, renewable energy; to increase energy efficiency; and to making energy affordable and reliable for everyone in the city," said Minneapolis Mayor Betsy Hodges. "This is a very promising solution that could be a model for cities across the nation to follow."

The partnership board is made up of two senior representatives from each utility, two city council members, the mayor, and the city coordinator. The board created an Energy Vision Advisory Committee (EVAC) to provide community feedback. The board began meeting in February, and named members of the advisory committee in March.

"CEE articulated a third way – by identifying the partnership – which wasn't part of the MEO plan," said Farrell. "By funding the study the city signaled their commitment to meeting climate goals, but they weren't sure about committing to municipalization. The city made it clear to the utilities that they were serious about the options. None of the options in the pathways study were the status quo."

"There was a big debate among advocates about whether we had won or lost," said Farrell. "The partnership set up a process to work on the issues, to give it a chance. I'm an optimist that the partnership might work."

Bradley seems more skeptical.

"Minneapolis has a notoriously slow bureaucracy," he said. "They urge the state and federal government to do things, but have a hard time looking at themselves to see what they can do."

"Cities all the time say they are going to do things, issue proclamations. A big plan is released, and usually only a tiny piece of it actually happens," he said. "I hope the city can be more functional this time."

Farrell, who is serving on the advisory committee to the partnership, is worried that the agreements being reached lack any teeth or accountability. The partnership released the first two-year work plan at the end of May.

"Now a year after the agreement some of our hopes are being realized and so are some of our worst fears," he said. "The new work plan has good language and programs but no metrics. Nothing about end goals or numbers."

For instance, the city has not created a new revenue source for programs, instead relying on existing resources and budgets. Whereas Boulder citizens imposed a carbon tax on themselves to fund their transition, Minneapolis has not taken that necessary step.

When the city council looked at the first budget to implement the program they considered cutting it well below proposed amounts. But a big turnout from the MEO campaign changed their minds.

Moreover, since Xcel's energy programs are funded by customers across the state, they will be unable to earmark funds solely for Minneapolis. Instead, Bull thinks the city can use local programs to drive greater participation in Xcel program offerings, which would drive additional resources into Minneapolis. Xcel can also test pilot programs in Minneapolis that could then be offered elsewhere in the state.

Xcel is also investigating changes to its business model, working in a stakeholder collaborative called e21. Initiated by the Great Plains Institute, e21 is studying changes to regulations that would "align an economically viable utility model with state and federal public policy goals."

The e21 effort is seeking ways to "offer customers more options in how and where their energy is produced and how and when they use it." More fundamentally, it is exploring ways to "shift away from a regulatory system that rewards the sale of electricity and building large, capital-intensive power plants and other facilities toward one that rewards utilities for achieving an agreed-upon set of performance outcomes that the public and customers want (e.g., energy efficiency, reliability, affordability, emissions reductions, predictable rates, etc.)."[39]

Such shifts would seemingly address the complaints of activists and city officials in Boulder, who blamed Xcel's business model more than the company itself. Xcel is seeking permission from Minnesota policymakers for the changes generated by the initiative.

Bull was working at Xcel Energy when the utility trade group EEI came out with the *Disruptive Challenges* report and plans to preserve their business model by fighting solar energy and imposing higher fixed charges. This approach concerned him. As long as Xcel profited by selling more power and building more power plants, it would be in conflict with what customers want, he told *Utility Dive*.[40]

"As new technologies become more cost-effective and available, it is inevitable that customers will want them," he said. "And it is a bad business practice for a utility or a regulator to get in the way of that."

Bull thinks state regulators will be comfortable with the changes implied by the Minneapolis Clean Energy Partnership and the e21 Initiative. "They are trying to be supportive of innovation, and are seeing this as an opportunity for innovation," he said.

Still, nothing is assured. "Right now the utilities seem completely committed, but that can change over time," he said. "And the same with the city council, which can change. The city needs to stay focused, or the utilities will stray."

"It's not just creating the want-to and the structures," he thinks. "It will take sustained focus over years."

Farrell, Bradley, and others haven't ruled out municipalization as a future option. "We holstered the gun," said Farrell, "but could use it again in the future."

Boulder response to Minneapolis

The reaction from Boulder to Minneapolis' agreement with Xcel has been mixed.

Boulder Mayor Matt Appelbaum told the *Daily Camera* that if Xcel had been willing to offer a shorter franchise agreement in 2010, Boulder and Xcel might have made more progress.

"We many times asked Xcel if they would work with us, if there could be a shorter franchise, if there could be opt-out provisions, and they said no, no, no," he said.[41]

To Jonathan Koehn, the Minneapolis agreement is the same as where Boulder was five years ago. They have created a committee to talk, but "there are no teeth, no performance measures."

Farrell partly disagrees, pointing to the shorter franchise agreement as the "linchpin" of the agreement, giving the city leverage and Xcel an incentive to follow through on the city's energy goals.

Farrell said activists had sought a two-year franchise in Minneapolis, but a five-year opt-out gives more time for Xcel to produce results.

"You can't turn a big corporate utility on a dime," he said. "We could probably evaluate the process after two years, but we couldn't evaluate outcomes in that time. Let's evaluate every year from year 4 to year 10. I'm optimistic that there are some really great ways we could work with the utility."

But Ken Regelson, an advocate of municipalization, sides with Koehn. "There is no 'there' there," he told the Daily Camera. "Xcel doesn't have to do anything. The only recourse [Minneapolis] has is to pull out. There is nothing there for Boulder. We've already gone through this long process trying to get something from Xcel and they've said, basically, 'Stick it in your ear.'"

"I expect they will be having the same conversation in five years – what are our options?" Koehn predicted. "Xcel's business model doesn't facilitate creativity and moving fast to sell less of their product."

Chapter 5:
The tale of Madison

The traditional utility business model, combined with incendiary state politics, is driving a similar kind of frustration in Wisconsin, though with a unique set of drivers and circumstances. Instead of seeking to adapt to changing times, Wisconsin utilities are doubling down on their business model, reinforcing it to prevent the kinds of innovation seen elsewhere in the United States.

Wisconsin utilities have done substantially less on global warming pollution than Xcel Energy, and if anything seem to be moving in the opposite direction.

The state renewable electricity standard, first adopted in 1999, is only 10 percent by 2015, one of the lowest of the 30 states with such standards, and it was met two years early. Utilities have no plans for further procurement of renewables, and the legislature is not considering extending and expanding the goal. Wisconsin used to be a national leader in energy efficiency, but are now ranked 17th by the ACEEE, trailing all of their neighboring states.

As they have for utilities in the rest of the country, carbon emissions in Wisconsin have fallen slightly as aging coal plants are pushed out by cheaper natural gas. But the state has no carbon reduction policies, and in fact is suing the EPA to block the Clean Power Plan, the first national effort to regulate global warming pollution from existing power plants.

Gov. Walker, at the time of this writing campaigning for president, slammed the rule when it came out. "President Obama's plan should be called the Costly Power Plan because it will cost hard-working Americans jobs and raise their energy rates," he said in a statement from his presidential campaign. "It will be like a buzz saw on the nation's economy. I will stand up for American workers and stop the Costly Power Plan."[42]

According to *The Coal Truth*, a recent report from the citizens' group RePower Madison, Madison Gas & Electric (MGE) has the highest commitment to coal – and the most expensive power – of any Wisconsin utility.[43] Fully half of the utility's power comes from the 40-year-old Columbia coal plant, which has racked up almost $1 billion in upgrades over the past decade.

Another quarter of MGE's supply comes from the Elm Road plant, which is co-owned with We Energies and the public power supplier WPPI. Built in 2010 at a price of $2.4 billion, it was the most expensive construction project in state history, and almost $200 million over budget.

Worse, the plant ran at only a quarter of capacity in 2013, producing electricity at an "all-in" cost of 14.76 cents per kWh – higher than the retail price of electricity. Yet because ratepayers can't choose their supplier in Wisconsin, they are stuck paying for this expensive and largely unneeded power plant, plus a 12.7 percent profit guaranteed by the state utility commission.

This has led to a steady rise in electricity rates for Wisconsin utilities. An average monthly bill has risen by about 25 percent since 2002, after adjusting for inflation, according to the Public Service Commission. MGE and We Energies have the highest bills by far of the state's five investor-owned utilities, and those bills are continuing to rise.

While all of these factors have led to some discontent, customer anger was really triggered by a set of proposals for the design of rates and the rules for customers generating their own power from solar panels.

As mentioned earlier, utilities across the country are discovering that the growth of distributed energy resources is posing a threat to their traditional business model. New technologies are allowing customers to use less energy and generate more of their own, driving down revenues for utilities. While some states are changing their rules to encourage innovation and tap the benefits of new technologies, Wisconsin regulators are doing the opposite.

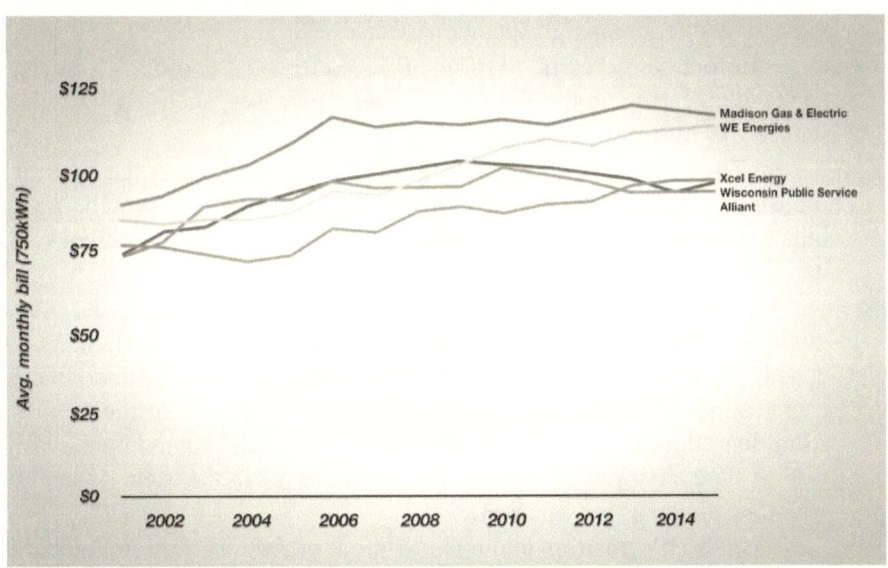

Figure 2: MGE and We Energies bills are the highest in the state (Source: Wisconsin PSC)

The utility pushback has been organized and led by their national trade association, the Edison Electric Institute. EEI and the utilities have been shopping for venues with friendly regulators and legislators. Wisconsin, under the Scott Walker administration, is extremely pro-business and anti-regulation, with strong ties to Koch-affiliated organizations.[44]

Walker's appointments at the state utility commission reflect this. Commissioner Phil Montgomery was the American Legislative Exchange Council's Legislator of the Year in 2005 and was active on the ALEC board until being appointed to the PSC. ALEC is a group that brings legislators and corporate lobbyists together to develop model bills "that reach into almost every area of American life and often directly benefit huge corporations." Funders include Koch Industries, ExxonMobil, and others.[45]

Montgomery's chief aide was R.J. Pirlot, previously the director of legislative relations at Wisconsin Manufacturers & Commerce, the state's largest business lobby.

Commissioner Ellen Nowak is a Republican operative with no energy background, but known as a school voucher champion. She was recently appointed chair of the commission.

She is served by the executive assistant, Bob Seitz, the past head of Wisconsin Utility Investors, the association of utility shareholders who push for higher utility profits. He is also the former lobbyist for Gogebic Taconite, which sought to build a highly controversial iron ore mine in northern Wisconsin, and which was at the center of a state investigation into alleged Walker campaign finance violations.[46]

Before being recruited for the PSC, Seitz – the corporate lobbyist – spoke at a hearing on the We Energies rate increases, accusing the solar industry of hurting the poor.[47]

"The insidious part of this big-money campaign from the rooftop solar industry is that they attempt to motivate those least able to pay their electric bills to fight for the most regressive subsidy of the wealthy I am aware of," he said.

The third commissioner, Eric Callisto, was appointed by the previous governor, Democrat Jim Doyle, and served until early 2015 when his term ended. To replace him, Walker appointed another loyalist with no energy background, Mike Huebsch, who was the head of the Department of Administration. Huebsch, described as Walker's "right-hand man," is also a former state chair of ALEC during his eight terms in the State Assembly, which he ended as the Speaker.

Huebsch's position at the Department of Administration, incidentally, was filled by an MGE executive, Scott Neitzel.

On June 10 last year, Commissioner Ellen Nowak spoke on a conference panel in Las Vegas with Gale Klappa, the CEO of We Energies' parent company WEPCO. Nowak urged utilities to request higher fixed charges on all customers, "so those customers who don't participate in [distributed generation] are not paying for those who do."[48]

Three weeks later, We Energies submitted to the PSC a detailed proposal for changes including the fixed charge increase, which makes solar much less viable. Similar proposals came from Wisconsin Public Service and MGE. In fact, MGE proposed raising its fixed charges from $10 to $69 a month, ramping up over three years.

While rate designs can vary by location and type of customer, a typical residential customer pays only for the amount of energy they consume each month, in the form of kilowatt-hours (kWh). In some states, regulators allow a small monthly fixed charge, typically $10 or less.

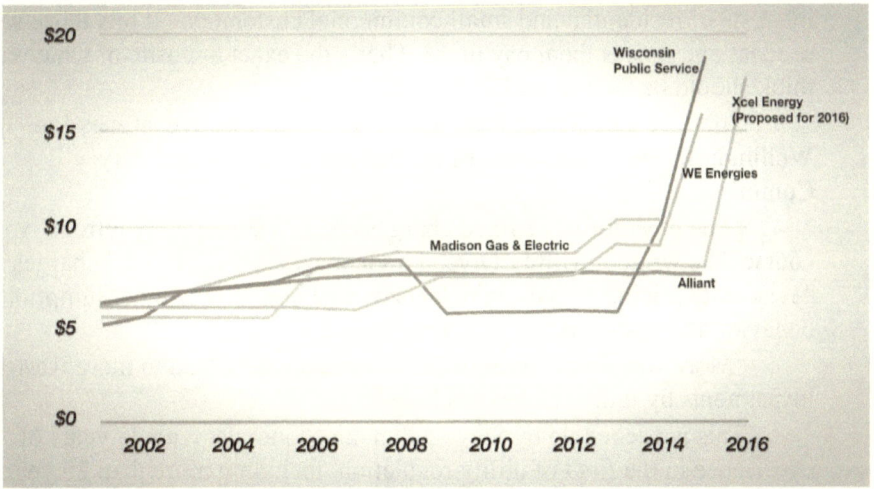

Figure 3: Meter fees on the rise. Wisconsin utilities charging more regardless of use. (Source: Wisconsin PSC)

This simple "volumetric" design allows utilities to cover their operating costs, while also encouraging customers to conserve energy. It is especially helpful for low-income and elderly customers, who can cut back on energy use to save money.

But flat demand for electricity combined with the increasing cost-effectiveness of solar power has convinced utilities that they need to make more money from fixed charges and less from kWh charges.

From the perspective of utilities, this is a great way to maintain utility profits.

First, it guarantees that utilities will keep making money no matter how little electricity their customers buy from them. By reducing risk, it allows them to borrow money at lower rates, which also increases profits.

Second, it discourages customers from producing their own power with solar panels, since the value of energy produced is lower and the payback period is longer. This keeps electricity sales high and eliminates a form of competition.

Third, it gives customers an incentive to consume more power, since the cost of each additional kWh is lower. Rising demand for power means utilities can build more power plants, increasing the guaranteed return they get from regulators.

But from the perspective of customers it is a disaster.

"Increasing fixed charges jacks up the cost of electricity for people in small apartments and those who are trying to conserve," said Kira Loehr, executive director of the Citizens Utility Board, which represents the interests of residential and small commercial customers. "It hits those who use less and makes them pay more. That's the exact opposite of what we think should be happening."[49]

They are also wrong from an economic perspective, argues Jon Wellinghoff, the former chair of the Federal Energy Regulatory Commission.[50]

"The push for more fixed charges charts a damagingly retroactive course," he wrote in Utility Dive, a trade magazine. High fixed charges "eviscerate pricing signals, which encourage both efficient consumption behavior and cost-effective grid investments."

"More wasteful consumer consumption would lead to more wasteful investments by utilities," he concluded.

This is backed up by Steve Kihm, an economist with 35 years of experience in the field of utility regulation, including more than 20 years as an analyst at the PSC.[51]

"There actually is no economic theory that supports recovery of fixed costs through fixed charges," he said. "High fixed charge pricing steers the economy away from efficient resource allocation, not toward it."

"In the long run, all costs are variable," he explained. "While increased electricity use does not affect the cost of existing capacity, it very well may affect the need for new capacity.

"Fixed charges tell consumers that if they use more electricity the utility will never have to add capacity. That is inaccurate."

The reaction to the rate proposals was strong and swift, especially in Madison, served by MGE, and Milwaukee, served by We Energies.

"This year's rate case has generated outcry like none other in recent years, including radio ads, videos for and against, and thousands of public comments," reported the Milwaukee *Journal Sentinel*. "More than 1,500 people had filed comments opposing and supporting the utility's plan – six times the number filed online just two years ago in a We Energies case."

Testimony on the charges ran overwhelmingly against, with only the utilities testifying in favor. Particularly strong opposition came from advocates for low income and senior customers, including the Dane County chapter of the NAACP, the state AARP, and the association of Community Action Agencies (WISCAP), which operate federal weatherization and energy assistance programs for the poor. They were joined by the cities of Madison, Fitchburg and Monona along with Dane County and others. Madison approved funding and hired an expert witness to intervene in the case. The Milwaukee Common Council issued a resolution opposing the changes.[52]

Opponents created RePower Madison and the Alliance for Fair Utilities in Milwaukee. The two groups rallied events, organized responses, and attracted over 1,000 social media followers. RePower Madison also helped launch and spin off a group, MGE Shareholders for Clean Energy, which drafted resolutions that would direct the utility to develop a plan for getting to 25 percent renewable energy by 2025 and tie executive compensation to achieving sustainability goals. The resolutions were withdrawn after MGE executives agreed to discuss it with the shareholder group.

Customer backlash to the proposal led MGE to negotiate with the Citizens Utility Board (CUB) to scale back its initial increase from $22 to $19 a month, hold the $69 charge for further discussion, and create a technical working group to study changes to the utility business model. Later, after customers picketed MGE headquarters, the utility agreed to start a public engagement process consisting of a series of town hall meetings.

MGE did not back down on its proposed increase to the fixed charge for natural gas service, raising it from $12 to $22 a month. Since MGE supplies both electricity and natural gas, fixed charges would rise from a combined $22 a month to $41 a month.

The rate cases were also caught up in broader political and ideological issues.

Americans for Prosperity, the political advocacy group founded by Charles and David Koch, weighed in in support of higher fixed charges, largely repeating the "fair share" talking points of EEI and We Energies.

"All should pay for their fair share of the electric grid," the group's state director, David Fladeboe, said in a memorandum.[53] "What solar advocates are pushing for would essentially force the rest of us without the means or desire to put solar panels on our roof or a wind turbine in our backyard to pay for their share of the grid. That's not fair and it's also not a free market."

They were countered by Barry Goldwater, Jr., a former Arizona Congressman and the son of the conservative Republican legend, and by Debbie Dooley, leader of the Atlanta-based Tea Party Patriots.

"Republicans want the freedom to make the best choice and the competition to drive down rates," Goldwater said. "We can't let solar energy – and all its advantages and benefits it provides us – be pushed aside by monopolies wanting to limit energy choice. That's not the conservative way and it's not the American way."[54]

Dooley, visiting Wisconsin, said "This is a referendum on free market conservatism. If you're a free-market conservative, you don't protect monopolies from competition, because the free market is all about competition."[55]

A surprise participant in the dockets was the Consumer Energy Alliance, a Houston-based group with strong connections to the fossil fuel industry.[56] They submitted a petition of Wisconsin citizens claiming to support the higher fixed charges and fees. But their involvement blew up when it was discovered the petition was fraudulent, full of names of people who denied having supported it. The petition was denied by the PSC, but no action was taken against the group for violating state law. Their funding for participation in the dockets is unknown, but some suspect it came from EEI. Utilities publicly distanced themselves from the group.

Another departure was that although regulatory proceedings usually hinge on evidence, with voluminous filings by lawyers, accountants, and engineers, the utilities presented very little analysis of the actual impact of solar and energy efficiency on rates.

Commissioner Callisto aired his frustrations in comments at a hearing on November 14.[57] "How can we be so sure of these supposed subsidies if we aren't willing to look at the costs and benefits?" he asked. "There is really no explanation for why we wouldn't take a good look at this. Virtually every other state is, yet here we are sticking our heads in the sand."

"I don't buy it."

Nevertheless, despite significant public opposition, the PSC awarded all the utilities big increases in fixed charges for customers, and an extra "solar tax" for solar customers of We Energies.[58]

There was a consensus among those interviewed that the outcome of the case was hardwired.

Brad Klein, attorney for the Environmental Law and Policy Center, said, "I've worked on utility cases for 10 years, and I've never seen a commission make a decision on a contested issue with less supporting evidence in the record."

Madison Mayor Paul Soglin also criticized the decision in a statement, saying it will "undermine energy conservation efforts, energy efficiency investments, and the renewable energy investments in our community."[59]

The decisions "protected a favored incumbent industry at the expense of household budgets, community health, and clean-energy innovation," wrote Raj Shukla, the chair of the city's Sustainable Madison Committee, in an op-ed.[60]

"MGE's new rates could increase pollution that causes climate change," Shukla wrote. "Instead of promoting clean-energy innovation, MGE doubles down on polluting fuels. Instead of driving efficiency, MGE makes it easier to waste. Instead of leadership, MGE has chosen denial."

We Energy's rate changes are even more severe than MGE's, and include extra fees and limits on customers with solar panels. WE's new rules impose an extra charge of about $180 a year just on solar customers, pay a lower rate for excess power generated during the day, eliminate the ability to roll over extra generation from month to month, and require customers to buy a second meter to monitor the solar system.[61]

Analysis by Renew Wisconsin estimates the changes will reduce a customer's return from a new solar system by 35 percent and cut savings from an existing system by 47 percent.[62]

"That would effectively demolish the economic appeal of rooftop solar. It would just take it away," said Michael Vickerman of Renew. "No other utility is trying as hard as We Energies is to deprive small customers of the option to self-generate with solar."

And the rate increases keep coming. In May, Xcel Energy, which serves parts of western Wisconsin, asked to increase fixed charges from $8 to $18 a month, the seventh straight year they have requested an electric rate increase.[63] For the smallest energy users, using 200 kWh per month – often low income and elderly customers – it would mean a 26 percent bigger bill. The biggest users – typically wealthier customers – would see an increase of only 2.2 percent. At the same time in Minnesota, Xcel requested that regulators increase their fixed charge from $8 to $9.25, but were turned down.[64]

Meanwhile, Wisconsin Public Service (WPS) has come back for another increase in monthly fixed charges, this time up to $25 a month.

The utilities and regulators both have noted the need to make the shift in costs gradual, presumably to prevent the full-on customer revolt that MGE experienced in Madison.

According to the Journal Sentinel, commissioners Phil Montgomery and Ellen Nowak said last year that "only the need for 'gradualism' prompted them to limit last year's increase to 83 percent." This year's increase for WPS would be an additional 36 percent.[65]

"WPS recognizes the need to realign rates with cost in a gradual manner over a number of rate cycles," said Ronda Ferguson, WPS regulatory affairs manager, in their filing.

Historical echoes in Madison

The current dispute between MGE and Madison citizens and officials has eerie echoes of a dispute over a century ago that led to the regulation of utilities in Wisconsin.

At the turn of the 20th century, Madison was the state capital and the home of the University, but was still only a small town of 20,000 people. Gov. "Fighting Bob" La Follette was a leader of the Progressives, a national movement devoted to breaking up big business "trusts," women's suffrage, and labor rights. Formed in 1896, the Madison Gas & Electric Company supplied power and gas, used for both heat and light.

By 1903, local citizens were outraged that MGE's gas prices were 25 percent higher than any other city in Wisconsin. "At the request of citizens of Madison the common council sought to compel the gas company to lower its rates," according to Fred L. Holmes, a former member of the state Assembly, writing in 1915.[66]

But MGE would not cooperate, refusing to share details of their costs. The city sued the utility, but lost the case in 1906 before the state supreme court, because there was no state legislation regulating how utilities could set rates.

Meanwhile, the university regents asked a professor to test the quality of MGE's gas on campus. "The professor discovered that 20 percent of the gas was nothing more than an inert element, nitrogen, which provided no light or heat but caused the meters to whirl just the same," according to David Mollenhoff, in a history of Madison.[67]

The Wisconsin State Journal called the utility "fraudulent" and began a muckraking crusade against the utility and its New York-based owners, the McMillan syndicate. They discovered that the utility had secretly offered a 53 percent cut in rates "to stave off a municipal takeover attempt in 1903," according to Mollenhoff.

"Occurring in the capital city of the state," Holmes wrote, "this case which showed the helplessness of a city to obtain just treatment for its citizens, aroused the feeling that culminated in enactment of the Public Utility Law of 1907."

UW professor John Commons drafted the law, which made Wisconsin the first state in the country to regulate electric and gas utilities.

"It was to escape the evils of local control that the Wisconsin Public Utility Law was enacted," Holmes wrote. Before the law citizens had to go to great lengths to appeal the actions of utilities through the courts.

"Most ordinary mortals, however, have neither the patience nor the funds with which to litigate with a large corporation, so they bear their little wrongs unremedied." A state commission, on the other hand, would have the resources and authority to ensure fair service. "Thus is the poor man given the aid of the state in remedying conditions, which otherwise he must shoulder or bear in silence."

Looking to Boulder and Minneapolis

RePower Madison was formed "as a reaction to the bad proposals," according to lead organizer Mitch Brey. "After that we looked at other communities like Boulder and Minneapolis, and saw places where the community is being heard and the utility is changing, either willingly or by force. It gave us inspiration that we could have something better here in Madison."

Madison and Milwaukee, like Boulder and Minneapolis, have aggressive climate goals as city policy. Both are seeking 25 percent of their power supply from renewable energy by 2025. Because the state renewable power standard has ended at 10 percent in 2015, the cities will need to make considerable progress on their own.

And these city sustainability goals are deeply out of sync with the actions of utilities and state regulators. Since a major portion of carbon emissions are embedded in the electricity and gas consumed by residents and businesses in the cities, it is virtually impossible for the goals to be met as long as decisions about the energy mix are out of cities' hands.

In Madison, Alderman David Ahrens played a key role in opposition to the fixed charge proposal, getting the city to intervene in the rate case, helping start RePower Madison, and winning unanimous support from the city council for the MGE shareholder resolutions.

He agrees that the state government will be of little help. On the contrary, he says, "the only matter is to what degree they will cripple all efforts at the local level."

Instead, Madison will have to seek cooperation directly with the utility. So far, the signs do not look promising.

"We want to look at alternative models for MGE," says Ahrens. "How do they reform themselves? Their only response so far is higher fixed rates. Is that economically feasible for low-income people to be stuck with that model? That was their initial proposal, which would have been catastrophic."

As in Boulder's experience, there is a track record of bad blood in Madison. In 2014, the City applied for a $600,000 grant from the U.S. Department of Energy to fund MadiSUN, a program to plan and encourage 60 MW of solar in Madison. There are currently about 2 MW of solar in MGE's service territory, which consumes about 800 MW of power.

In a letter supporting the application, Mayor Paul Soglin underscored the importance of local action. "Today in Wisconsin the responsibility for promoting clean energy has become the domain of cities. At least for now, the State of Wisconsin, once a leader in developing policies and funding mechanisms to support renewable energy, has retreated from this role."[68]

But MGE opposed the application, ensuring its rejection by DOE. MGE claimed the project would have "large technical and grid reliability impacts, which require a comprehensive engineering study."

They instead want to put off the discussion about solar until after community meetings are held. "We're going to discuss what type of renewables and how much generation from renewables MGE should be considering in its planning," spokesperson Steve Kraus told *The Isthmus*. "Until these conversations are completed, we're going to wait to make any future decisions."

Ahrens accused the utility of intentionally scuttling the grant application. "They wrote a nasty letter to DOE, that said the city was getting into their business," he recalled. "No one should do it but us. Anybody else is an intruder into our monopoly."

"Basically, 'you're the enemy, pal.'"

Ahrens contrasts this with MGE's image as "your community energy company," the company's slogan.

"They have spent a lot of money on their image, as a 'leading green corporation.' The greenwash is endless," Ahrens says. "But the Coal Truth report was a reality check, that MGE is not a green corporation."

In Madison, the growing pressure led MGE to schedule a series of Community Energy Conversations, small group meetings leading to larger meetings in the fall. The process "will involve many people and groups in an effort to help MGE define direction and priorities to serve this community going forward as a 'utility of the future.'"

Echoing the e21 Initiative in Minnesota, they have also established a Technical Work Group with the Citizens Utility Board and Clean Wisconsin, and support and guidance from the Great Plains Institute "to begin identifying options to address some key issues."

At the same time, meetings are under way between MGE management and shareholders in response to the shareholder resolutions.

Further change could come from the Madison city council, which asked the Sustainable Madison Committee to develop a plan for cutting electricity demand 50 percent by 2030 and getting 25 percent of city power from renewable energy by 2025. The committee will "investigate all options, including legal, statutory, and regulatory alternatives" for implementing the work plan, and a "framework for participating in MGE's community-wide conversations."[70]

Mitch Brey of RePower Madison has guarded hopes for the process, calling it a "once in a lifetime opportunity." In his view, "The utility of the future won't charge high fixed fees, they will make plans to increase clean energy, and be on the path to get away from carbon-based fuels, because that is what the future needs."

"But how can we be a leader in clean energy when our utility is so reliant on coal?" he asked.

Ahrens thinks MGE is facing inexorable change. "Popular will, market forces, and technology change will force a change in the way they do business," he said. "Or they will use the political process to squeeze us, and see how long they can play that out."

"Hopefully MGE is willing to go all the way," said Brey. "If not, the community is poised to go in its own direction, to get a utility interested in reducing carbon emissions."

"If it doesn't lead to substantial change, we'll have to figure out how to get our voice back," he cautioned. "The future shouldn't be left up to utility executives, since it really affects everyone's lives."

Chapter 6:
Tales yet to be written

We Energies has no plans for a similar engagement with officials or residents in Milwaukee, even as the city explores its own alternatives, at the urging of Alderman Robert Bauman.

The Milwaukee council approved a resolution last September directing staff to push for state legislation "to allow the city to expand retail choice for utility customers and expand competition within the energy industry by offering customers the opportunity to purchase energy from their current utility or an alternative supplier." It would also allow the city to be the group buyer for citizens and businesses; in other words, community choice aggregation.[71]

The council had earlier directed the city staff to develop an energy independence plan to reduce reliance on We Energies for city facilities.

"As I started to look at the full relationship between We Energies and the city, it began to become increasingly apparent that they're no longer a regulated monopoly," Bauman told the Shepherd Express. "They're just an outright monopoly."[72]

"Clearly we do not have a utility that is regulated in the public interest anymore," he said. "Their lobbyists literally brag about basically controlling the Public Service Commission through a three-member body appointed by the governor. They like to brag about controlling the legislature in terms of preventing any sort of statutory or regulatory changes that would rein in their rate increases. And now they're even going to actively discourage conversion to solar power."

"Clearly something has to give in this relationship with the utility and the city of Milwaukee, because they've become an active impediment to one of our economic development issues."

"There seems to be an argument there for government ownership of some of these utilities. There are some municipalities that do own their own utilities. So it's not an unheard-of notion, an unheard of concept."

We Energies' rate proposal had also drawn an especially pointed response from the Milwaukee Metropolitan Sewage District (MMSD). In an op-ed in the Journal Sentinel, Kevin Shafer, the executive director of MMSD, suggested "It may be time for sewerage district to unplug from We Energies."[73]

"This rate increase will force MMSD to seriously look at generating all of our own power and unplugging from We Energies," he wrote. "We've just started a long-range planning effort to decide our capital improvement needs to protect the environment, and unplugging from We Energies has moved to the front of this effort."

The commission ultimately did not approve the extra charges for the Milwaukee sewage district, but did apply them to residential customers.

That outcome shows that city-level action can be effective leverage.

Ursula Schryver of the American Public Power Association (APPA) sees a growing interest in local action to take greater control, including municipalization.

"Boulder has definitely brought it into the limelight and made more communities aware of the fact that they could pursue this," Schryver told Government Executive. "All of these speak to the fact that public power is all about local control. It allows cities to undertake projects that are of interest to the community."

There are over 2,000 utilities owned by various government bodies, such as cities and towns, public power districts, and state and federal governments. Some of the largest include Los Angeles, Seattle, San Antonio, and the Tennessee Valley Authority. There are also almost 900 cooperative utilities, owned by their customers, typically in rural areas. Altogether, these public utilities serve about 26 million customers, or 30 percent of the country.

More local communities are finding ways to get involved in cleaning up our energy system. Some community initiatives include:

• Santa Fe, New Mexico: The city has commissioned a study and is taking further steps necessary to buy the local grid from the investor-owned utility PNM to create Santa Fe Public Power, a municipal utility.

• Grand Rapids, Michigan: Under the leadership of Mayor George Hartwell, Grand Rapids has set a goal of 100 percent renewable energy by 2020, repowered all city lights with high-efficiency LEDs, and is developing a downtown "energy district" with buildings that use half the energy of conventional buildings. The city has been recognized by the United Nations, the U.S. Chamber of Commerce, and the U.S. Conference of Mayors.

• Community choice aggregation in California, Illinois, and Ohio: Communities in these states are allowed to aggregate the electricity demand of their residents and take bids from competitive power suppliers. It is sometimes called "muni-lite" since it doesn't involve creating a municipal utility or owning power equipment. Hundreds of cities and counties in these states have chosen CCA, especially in Illinois, where over 80 percent of residential customers are served by CCA contracts.

• Cincinnati, Ohio: By using CCA, Cincinnati chose a power supply that is 100 percent renewable, at a cost similar to conventional power supply.

• C40: The C40 Cities Climate Leadership Group is a network of the world's largest cities, including 13 in the United States, taking action to reduce greenhouse gas emissions.

• The City Energy Project: Ten U.S. cities are working to reduce energy use in buildings, with support from the Natural Resources Defense Council and the Institute for Market Transformation.

• Georgetown University Energy Prize: Fifty cities in 26 states, including Madison, are competing to reduce electricity and gas consumption over a two-year period. The winner receives $5 million.

• Take Charge Challenge: This Kansas initiative works with communities to challenge each other to increase energy efficiency.

Chapter 7:
Epilogue

The tale of these three cities – Boulder, Minneapolis, and Madison – has a common thread: utilities out of step with the communities they serve. The citizens and elected leaders of these communities are taking climate change seriously, and utility executives don't appreciate that fact.

It should be a cautionary tale for utility executives.

They spend much time exerting influence over state and federal officials and policies, trying to tamp down drastic change and preserve the status quo. But the more they do so, the more likely they are to foment a grassroots rebellion.

When state and national officials are afraid or unwilling to act, local communities can be inspired to action on their own.

While these cities don't have the immediate regulatory leverage of states, they are not without means – or the ability to acquire the means. Putting conditions on franchise agreements, taxes and fees, and full-on municipalization are all tools that can be deployed now. Local officials can also be influential advocates at state and federal forums, as well as in the court of public opinion. And they often go on to higher office, taking their past experience with them.

Recalcitrant utilities also face direct rebellion from customers. New technologies are offering a pathway for motivated customers to cut the cable altogether. As utilities try to stifle rooftop solar through higher fees, it merely gives customers more incentive to marry efficient homes with solar and increasingly affordable batteries, such as those offered by Elon Musk's Tesla. In the same way cell phones killed wired phones, energy self-reliant customers may no longer need to send any money to electric utilities.

The tale could also be inspiring to citizens and communities who want faster action on climate change, local control, or equity. Although many obstacles stand in the way, it is possible to create change.

And change is possible at the state level too, in different ways. Many states are eagerly encouraging energy efficiency and renewable energy, for economic development and job creation, to reduce fuel imports, and to solve environmental problems.

Even in less progressive states, the trend in the world of electricity policy is toward competition and choice. As clean energy becomes more competitive and more customers demand it (or demand to be allowed to choose it) barriers will fall.

Changing state policy is hardest in states where monopoly utilities have a lock on the political process, as in Wisconsin. Here local action is the only option, and the Tale of Three Cities could offer the most inspiration.

As Dickens said, this is both "the age of wisdom" and "the age of foolishness." But a revolution is brewing. Civic leaders and citizen activists in Boulder, Minneapolis, and Madison are working to "see a beautiful city and a brilliant people rising from this abyss."

References

Chapter 2

1. Meg Jones and Don Behm, Journal Sentinel, "Bluff collapse at power plant sends dirt, coal ash into lake," Oct. 31, 2011, http://www.jsonline.com/news/milwaukee/authorities-investigate-bluff-collapse-at-we-energies-plant-132929538.html.

2. Curtis Tate, McLatchy DC, "EPA: Illinois oil train derailment threatens Mississippi River," March 7, 2015, http://www.mcclatchydc.com/news/nation-world/national/economy/article24781141.html.

3. US Geological Survey, "Induced Earthquakes," http://earthquake.usgs.gov/research/induced/

4. Thomas Content, Journal Sentinel, "Wisconsin's frac sand industry booms," May 28, 2015, http://www.jsonline.com/business/wisconsins-frac-sand-industry-booms-b99509220z1-305394131.html

5. Steven Mufson and Juliet Eilperin, Washington Post, "The biggest foreign lease holder in Canada's oil sands isn't Exxon Mobil or Chevron. It's the Koch brothers", March 20, 2014, http://www.washingtonpost.com/news/wonkblog/wp/2014/03/20/the-biggest-land-owner-in-canadas-oil-sands-isnt-exxon-mobil-or-conoco-phillips-its-the-koch-brothers/

6. Richard Mial, LaCrosse Tribune, "Refinery takes Canadian oil and turns it into gasoline for Wisconsin," March 08, 2010, http://lacrossetribune.com/news/%20local/article_e76ad10e-2a6d-11df-8363-001cc4c002e0.html

7. Spencer Weart, American institute of Physics, The Discovery of Global Warming, February 2015, http://www.aip.org/history/climate/index.htm

8. Daniel J. Weiss, Center for American Progress, Anatomy of a Senate Climate Bill Death, October 12, 2010. https://www.americanprogress.org/issues/green/news/2010/10/12/8569/anatomy-of-a-senate-climate-bill-death/

9. US Environmental Protection Agency, "Clean Power Plan," http://www2.epa.gov/cleanpowerplan

10. Mitch McConnell, Lexington Herald Leader, Op-ed: "States should reject Obama mandate for clean-power regulations," March 3, 2015, http://www.kentucky.com/2015/03/03/3725288_states-should-reject-obama-mandate.html

11. E&E News, "Legal Challenges – Overview & Documents," http://www.eenews.net/interactive/clean_power_plan/fact_sheets/legal

12. Nicholas Confessore, New York Times, "Koch Brothers' Budget of $889 Million for 2016 Is on Par With Both Parties' Spending," January 26, 2015. http://www.nytimes.com/2015/01/27/us/politics/kochs-plan-to-spend-900-million-on-2016-campaign.html

13. Paul Waldman, Washington Post, "Where the 2016 GOP contenders stand on climate change," May 12, 2014, http://www.washingtonpost.com/blogs/plum-line/wp/2014/05/12/where-the-2016-gop-contenders-stand-on-climate-change/

14. DeSmog Blog, "Who is Donor's Trust?" http://www.desmogblog.com/who-donors-trust

15. US Energy Information Administration, Annual Energy Outlook 2015, April 14, 2015, http://www.eia.gov/forecasts/aeo/executive_summary.cfm

16. EEI, Disruptive Challenges: Financial Implications and Strategic Responses to a Changing Retail Electric Business, January 2013, http://www.eei.org/ourissues/finance/documents/disruptivechallenges.pdf

17. Evan Wyloge, Arizona Capitol Times, "APS: $9 million spent on net metering, energy deregulation PR," November 4, 2013, http://azcapitoltimes.com/news/2013/11/04/arizona-public-service-aps-spent-9-million-dollars-on-solar-net-metering-and-deregulation-public-relations/#ixzz3dXwTjFM0

Chapter 3

18. Heather Bailey, https://www.youtube.com/watch?v=0iaRKZ5FrZg

19. SWEEP, Utility Energy Efficiency Programs in Colorado: A Success Story, April 2014, http://www.swenergy.org/publications/factsheets/CO_DSM_factsheet_Apr2014.pdf

20. ACEEE, The State Energy Efficiency Scorecard, 2014 http://aceee.org/files/pdf/state-sheet/colorado.pdf

21. Xcel Energy, http://www.xcelenergy.com/Company/Operations/Power_Generation_Fuel_Mix_-_PSCo

22. Benchmarking Air Emissions, Natural Resources Defense Council, May 2014, http://www.nrdc.org/air/pollution/benchmarking/files/benchmarking-2014.pdf

23. City of Boulder, https://bouldercolorado.gov/energy-future/coal-carbon-intensity

24. Annie Lappe, Vote Solar, "Xcel Energy Puts Rooftop Solar in Jeopardy in Colorado," July 29, 2013. http://votesolar.org/2013/07/29/xcel-energy-puts-rooftop-solar-in-jeopardy-in-colorado/

25. David O. Williams, "In Electricity War, it's Boulder vs. Xcel Energy," Government Executive, July 14, 2014. http://www.govexec.com/state-local/2014/07/boulder-colorado-xcel-energy-utility-municipalization/88612/

26. Your CAP Tax Dollars At Work: Programs At-A-Glance, City of Boulder, https://www-static.bouldercolorado.gov/docs/Programs_At-a-Glance_v04_Final-1-201307081502.pdf

27. RW Beck, Preliminary Municipalization Feasibility Study, October 2005, https://www-static.bouldercolorado.gov/docs/2005_Beck-1-201306171525.pdf

28. Mark Jaffe, "Xcel's SmartGridCity plan fails to connect with Boulder," The Denver Post, October 28, 2012, http://www.denverpost.com/ci_21871552/xcels-smartgridcity-plan-fails-connect-boulder

29. Xcel Energy, "What's the Cost of Municipalization?", October 2, 2011, https://www.xcelenergy.com/staticfiles/xe/Corporate/Corporate%20PDFs/Final_11%2008x10_Daily_Camera_oct2.pdf

30. Cathy Proctor, "Xcel willing to sell wholesale power to breakaway Boulder utility, but wants more talks first," Denver Business Journal, May 19, 2015, http://www.bizjournals.com/denver/blog/earth_to_power/2015/05/xcel-willing-to-sell-wholesale-power-to-breakaway.html

31. Jaclyn Brandt, "Boulder needs Xcel's help to transition to clean energy," Fierce Energy, April 20, 2015, http://www.fierceenergy.com/story/boulder-needs-xcels-help-transition-clean-energy/2015-04-20

32. Proctor, Denver Business Journal, ibid

Chapter 4

33. U.S. Conference of Mayors, http://www.usmayors.org/climateprotection/agreement.htm

34. Erica Meltzer, "Former Boulder mayor talks municipalization in Xcel's hometown in Minnesota," Daily Camera, September 25, 2012. http://www.dailycamera.com/ci_21630267/former-boulder-mayor-talks-municipalization-xcels-hometown-minnesota

35. City of Minneapolis Energy Vision 2014, released September 3, 2013, https://cleanenergypartnership.files.wordpress.com/2014/12/mpls-energy-vision-9-3-13.pdf

36. Energy Pathways Study, http://www.ci.minneapolis.mn.us/energyfranchise/WCMS1P-113782

37. LEAN Energy U.S., http://www.leanenergyus.org/cca-by-state/illinois/

38. Minneapolis Clean Energy Partnership, http://mplscleanenergypartnership.org

39. Great Plains Institute, e21 Initiative, http://www.betterenergy.org/projects/e21-initiative.

40. Herman K. Trabish, Utility Dive, "How the e21 Initiative is building smarter utility business models in Minnesota," June 18, 2015, http://www.utilitydive.com/news/how-the-e21-initiative-is-building-smarter-utility-business-models-in-minne/400781/

41. Erica Meltzer, Daily Camera, October 25, 2014, "Boulder example 'hung over' Minneapolis negotiations with Xcel Energy," http://www.dailycamera.com/news/boulder/ci_26798190/boulder-example-hung-over-minneapolis-negotiations

Chapter 5

42. Jessie Opoien, The Capital Times, "Scott Walker slams Obama administration's Clean Power Plan," August 03, 2015, http://host.madison.com/news/local/govt-and-politics/election-matters/scott-walker-slams-obama-administration-s-clean-power-plan/article_10da19c2-c0e0-5f7d-89ce-781421ccf3fb.html

43. Peter Taglia, RePower Madison, The Coal Truth, http://www.repowermadison.org/wp-content/uploads/2015/05/Coal-Truth-Report.pdf

44. Kira Lerner, Think Progress, "Why the Koch Brothers Want Scott Walker to be President," April 21, 2015, http://thinkprogress.org/election/2015/04/21/3649458/koch-scott-walker-endorsement/

45. Center for Media and Democracy, ALEC Exposed, http://www.alecexposed.org/wiki/ALEC_Exposed.

46. Editorial board, New York Times, "How to Buy a Mine in Wisconsin," August 31, 2014. http://www.nytimes.com/2014/09/01/opinion/did-gov-scott-walker-violate-campaign-laws.html

47. Kari Lydersen, Midwest Energy News, "In Milwaukee, critics blast We Energies rate proposal," October 9, 2014, http://www.midwestenergynews.com/2014/10/09/in-milwaukee-critics-blast-we-energies-rate-proposal-wisconsin-solar/

48. Chris Martin, "Wisconsin Utility Sought Solar Fees After Regulator Advised CEO," Bloomberg Business, November 24, 2014, http://www.bloomberg.com/news/articles/2014-11-24/wisconsin-utility-sought-solar-fees-after-regulator-advised-ceo

49. Chris Hubbuch, LaCrosse Tribune, "Xcel seeks to raise fixed cost for electricity use," May 29, 2015, http://lacrossetribune.com/news/local/xcel-seeks-to-raise-fixed-cost-for-electricity-use/article_6bb617e2-6253-53fd-ad15-fda1a07d4d29.html.

50. James Tong and Jon Wellinghoff, Utility Dive, "Why fixed charges are a false fix to the utility industry's solar chal- lenges," February 13, 2015, http://www.utilitydive.com/news/tong-and-wellinghoff-why-fixed-charges-are-a-false-fix-to-the-utility-indu/364428/

51. Steve Kihm, 2015, "Economic concerns about high fixed charge pricing for electric service," http://americaspowerplan.com/wp-content/uploads/2014/10/Economic-analysis-of-high-fixed-charges.pdf.

52. See http://city.milwaukee.gov/ImageLibrary/Groups/ccCouncil/2014-PDF/January/District04/04-CouncilapprovesWeEnergiesfi.pdf

53. David Fladeboe, state director, Americans for Prosperity – Wisconsin, "All Should Pay for Their Fair Share of the Electric Grid," September 15, 2014. http://americansforprosperity.org/wisconsin/article/memo-all-should-pay-for-their-fair-share-of-the-electric-grid/

54. Tell Utilities Solar Won't be Killed, http://dontkillsolar.com/tusk/.

55. Thomas Content, Journal Sentinel, "Tea party official rips We Energies' plan to alter solar charges," September 16, 2014.

56. Mike Ivey, The Capital Times, "PSC tosses out petition supporting MGE rate hike," October 30, 2014, http://host.madison.com/news/local/writers/mike_ivey/psc-tosses-out-petition-supporting-mge-rate-hike/article_04e6e576-605e-11e4-a6e7-1353b30bf982.html#ixzz3dMJkMUGG

57. RePower Madison, PSC Commissioner Callisto on Plans for Increased Fixed Charges (audio recording), November 14, 2014, http://www.repowermadison.org/psc-commissioner-callisto-on-fixed-charges/

58. On utilities and solar, Wisconsin goes its own way, Midwest Energy News, December 3, 2014.

59. Mike Ivey, The Capital Times, "MGE rate hike approval draws fire," November 27, 2014, http://host.madison.com/news/local/writers/mike_ivey/mge-rate-hike-approval-draws-fire/article_cb49c470-75aa-11 e4-8bdf-3b1721258cb5.html#ixzz3dMFNQDJO

60. Raj Shukla: Madison should pursue new energy options, The Capital Times, December 3, 2014. http://host.madison.com/news/opinion/column/raj-shukla-madison-should-pursue-new-energy-options/article_cd7eab82-3791-504d-bd5a-0fb7785e7fd8.html#ixzz3c8JIl8Kr

61. City of Milwaukee analysis, http://city.milwaukee.gov/sustainability/Residents/EnergyEngagement.htm.

62. Robert Walton, Utility Dive, "Activists say We Energies' rate plan would 'effectively demolish' rooftop solar," October 28, 2014, http://www.utilitydive.com/news/activists-say-we-energies-rate-plan-would-effectively-demolish-rooftop-s/326492/

63.Chris Hubbuch, LaCrosse Tribune, "Xcel seeks to raise fixed cost for electricity use," May 29, 2015, http://lacrossetribune.com/news/local/xcel-seeks-to-raise-fixed-cost-for-electricity-use/article_6bb617e2-6253-53fd-ad15-fda1a07d4d29.html

64. Kari Lydersen, Midwest Energy News, Will Minnesota fixed-rate decision impact Wisconsin fight?, April 15, 2015.

http://www.midwestenergynews.com/2015/04/15/will-minnesota-fixed-rate-decision-impact-wisconsin-fight/

65. Thomas Content, Journal Sentinel, May 18, 2015

66. Fred L. Holmes, Regulation of Railroads and Public Utilities in Wisconsin, D. Appleton & Co., 1915, on Google Books at http://bit.ly/1JqLQ1p.

67. David Mollenhoff, Madison: A History of the Formative Years, Second edition, University of Wisconsin Press, 2003

68. "Soglin Letter to USDOE Re MadiSUN 071114," posted by The Isthmus, http://www.scribd.com/doc/243012323/Soglin-Letter-to-USDOE-Re-MadiSUN-071114.

69. Joe Tarr, The Isthmus, "MGE opposes Madison's effort to grow solar energy," October 15, 2014, http://www.isthmus.com/news/news/mge-opposes-madisons-effort-to-grow-solar-energy/#sthash.ru6AUC4n.dpuf

70. Madison Common Council, Resolution RES-15-00313, March 31, 2015, https://madison.legistar.com

Chapter 6

71. Milwaukee Common Council press release, "Council approves scrutiny of We Energies' acquisition, weighs in on deregulation," September 23, 2014, http://city.milwaukee.gov/ImageLibrary/Groups/ccCouncil/2014-PDF/January/District04/04-CouncilapprovesWeEnergiesfi.pdf

72. Louis Fortis, Shepherd Express, "Milwaukee Alderman Bob Bauman Speaks Out on the City's Future," July 30, 2014, http://shepherdexpress.com/article-permalink-23730.html

73. Kevin Shafer, Journal Sentinel, Op-ed: "It may be time for sewerage district to unplug from We Energies," October 24, 2014, http://www.jsonline.com/news/opinion/it-may-be-time-for-sewerage-district-to-unplug-from-we-energies-b99376394z1-280373622.html

www.ingramcontent.com/pod-product-compliance
Lightning Source LLC
Chambersburg PA
CBHW021923170526
45157CB00005B/2161